Mechanic Mike's Machines

Farm Machines

W
FRANKLIN WATTS
LONDON•SYDNEY

First published in the UK in 2014 by Franklin Watts

Franklin Watts
338 Euston Road
London NW1 3BH

Franklin Watts
Level 17/207 Kent Street
Sydney, NSW 2000

Dewey classification: 631.3

A CIP catalogue record for this book is available from the British Library.

ISBN: 978 1 4451 2724 8

Franklin Watts is a division of Hachette Children's Books, an Hachette UK company.
www.hachette.co.uk

MECHANIC MIKE'S MACHINES FARM MACHINES
was produced for Franklin Watts by
David West Children's Books, 6 Princeton Court, 55 Felsham Road, London SW15 1AZ

Copyright © 2014 David West Children's Books

Designed and illustrated by David West

Printed in China

Mechanic Mike says:
Mike will tell you
something more about
the machine.

Find out what type
of engine drives
the machine.

Discover
something you
didn't know.

When was it
invented or who
invented it?

What did we do
before it was
invented?

Get your
amazing
fact here!

Contents

Mechanic Mike says:
Most tractors have a power **take-off shaft** at the back. This transfers power from the tractor's engine to the machine it is towing, such as a baler or a mower.

Tractor

The busiest machine on a farm is the tractor. They are used for many jobs such as pulling trailers, cultivators, planters and balers. The engine provides power to all of the four large wheels to give extra grip.

The largest tractor is the Challenger MT975B. It weighs just over 24.49 metric tons.

The first tractors appeared about 1850. They were steam-powered ploughing engines. In 1892 John Froelich invented and built the first gas-powered tractor in Iowa, USA.

Did you know that Henry Ford made the first mass-produced tractor in 1917? It was called the Fordson.

Before tractors were invented, pulling was done by oxen and large, powerful horses.

Modern farm tractors usually use **diesel engines**.

Mechanic Mike says:
Modern cultivators are used
after the soil has been ploughed.

Power take-off shaft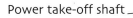

Cultivator

Fields are prepared for planting
with a cultivator. It is towed
behind a tractor. The discs and spiked
wheels turn the soil over, getting air
into it, and pulling up weeds.

Cultivators vary a lot in width, from 3 metres to 24 metres wide.

Ploughs pulled by oxen were used more than 3,000 years ago in ancient Egypt.

Did you know that drought and deep ploughing turned prairie land to dust in America and Canada in the 1930s? It was called the 'Dust Bowl'.

In ancient times preparing the soil was done by hand, with ploughs and hoes. Early ploughs and cultivators were pulled by animals such as horses, mules or oxen.

Cultivators are powered by the tractor's engine via a power take-off shaft.

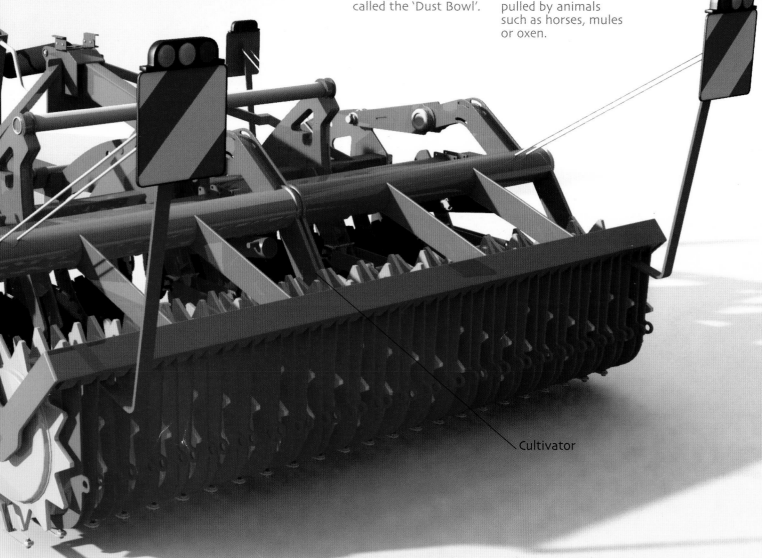

Cultivator

Spreader

This machine is used for spreading seeds or fertiliser. Seeds or pellets of fertiliser are dropped onto spinning discs, which scatter them onto the soil.

Large broadcast spreaders can spread seeds across widths of up to 27 metres.

Did you know that some spreaders are made for garden-size tractors and use a 2-volt motor to power the spinning disc?

Mechanical spreaders were invented in the late 1800s.

Seeds used to be spread by hand as the farmer walked up and down the field.

Broadcast spreaders are powered by the tractor's engine via a power take-off shaft.

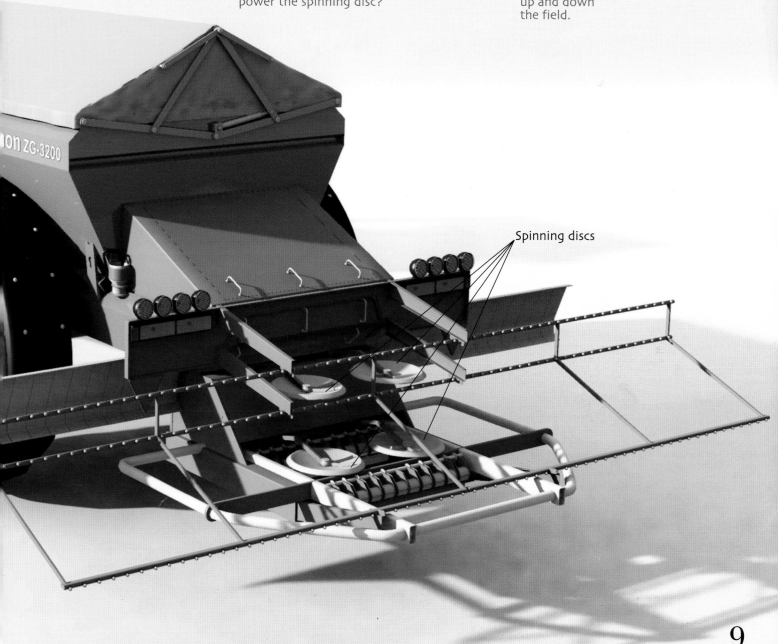

on ZG·3200

Spinning discs

9

Planter

Planters are towed
behind a tractor to
sow crops through a field.
They lay the seed down in rows
in a very precise pattern.

Planters vary in size from just 2 rows to the biggest in the world, which has 48 rows.

Henry Blair invented the seed planter in 1834, so that farmers could plant more corn, more quickly, using less labour. The wheeled machine was pulled by a horse.

Before the invention of the seed planter a farmer had to plant seeds by hand.

Did you know that satellite navigation and automatic steering for the tractor are often used to make sure the seeds are planted accurately?

Planters are powered by the tractor's engine via a power take-off shaft.

Mechanic Mike says:
Planting machines, such as rice planters, take the back-breaking work out of the process. But it is still done by hand in some places, especially in small rice paddy fields.

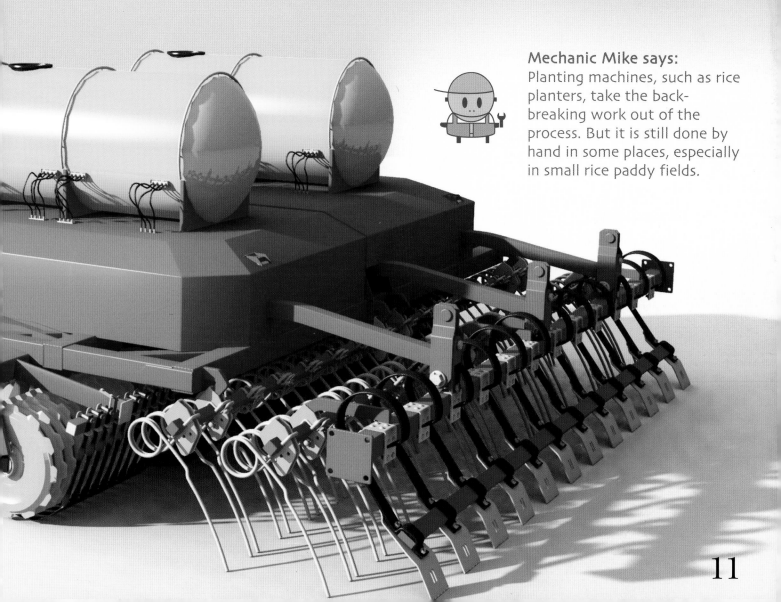

11

Harvester

This combine harvester is one of many different types of harvesters. It combines the three separate operations of reaping, threshing and winnowing into one process.

Mechanic Mike says:
First, the combine cuts the crop (reaping). Secondly, it loosens the edible part of the grain or seeds from the rest of the plant (threshing). Thirdly, it separates the grain or seeds from the husks and straw (winnowing).

12

Auger

Crops harvested with a combine include wheat, oats, rye, barley, corn, soya beans and flax.

Combine harvesters are powered by diesel engines.

Before the combine was invented, reaping, threshing and winnowing were all done by hand.

Did you know there are also harvesting machines that collect cotton, grapes, potatoes and peas?

The combine was invented in the United States by Hiram Moore in 1834 and early versions were pulled by horses or mules.

Grain carts can carry around 15 metric tons. The largest can carry 50 metric tons. That's the weight of about 25 cars!

Carts have been used to transport grain since ancient times.

Grain was originally collected in bags that weighed 109 kilogrammes. These were lifted by hand onto a **horse-drawn** cart.

Did you know grain carts are also called grain wagons? They allow the harvester machine to operate continually without stopping to unload.

If the grain cart has an auger it is powered by the tractor via a power take-off shaft.

Mechanic Mike says
Grain carts are used to transport the grain or corn over the fields from a combine harvester to a **semi-trailer truck**, which then drives the longer distances by road.

14

Grain Cart

As a combine moves along it is accompanied by a grain cart, pulled by a tractor. The grain from the combine is poured into the cart using an auger.

Mechanic Mike says:
Balers produce bales of hay in a rectangle or cylinder shape. This one makes rectangular bales.

Baler

After the harvester has finished, the leftover stalks that lie on the ground are collected, compressed into bales of hay and bound with twine.

Rectangular bales are easier to transport and don't roll away on hillsides.

Did you know some hay is stored in silos? This hay is much wetter than hay bales and turns to silage. Silage is used as food for cattle.

In 1872 a reaper that used a knotter device to bundle and bind hay was invented by Charles Withington.

Before the 19th century, hay was cut by hand and usually stored in haystacks.

Balers are powered by the tractor's engine via a power take-off shaft.

Stacker

Bales of hay are picked up from the field and stacked onto trailers by a self-powered machine called a bale stacker.

Mechanic Mike says:
The pallet fork at the front of the stacker's arm can be swapped for other devices, such as a feed bucket, to allow it to perform other tasks.

Pallet fork

Some balers use an automated device that throws the hay bale into the wagon behind it.

Automated devices for stacking bales as they leave the baler have been used for a few decades.

Before automated devices, teams of workers would grab bales with sharp metal hooks and throw them onto a flatbed wagon. A worker on the wagon stacked the bales.

Did you know weights have to be added to the back of the stacker to stop it tipping forwards when it lifts heavy loads?

Bale stackers use diesel engines.

Mechanic Mike says:
The front arm crops hay from bales. Augers carry the hay up the arm into the mixer. Here it is mixed with protein supplements, minerals and vitamins to make the **Total Mixed Ration**.

 The Total Mixed Ration is distributed from a side chute as the machine drives along.

? Computers control the mixture of the Total Mixed Ration.

💡 The self-propelled mixer feeder was invented in the 1980s.

Before automated mixers cattle feed was mixed by hand.

Mixer

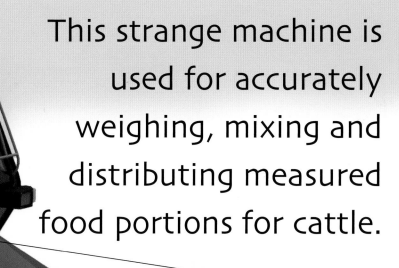

This strange machine is used for accurately weighing, mixing and distributing measured food portions for cattle.

Auger

Mixer wagons are powered by diesel engines.

Transport

Farmers use special vehicles to carry themselves and their animals. **4x4** pickup trucks are used to get around and to tow small trailers, such as horse trailers.

Mechanic Mike says:
Pickup trucks are an ideal form of transport on large farms as they can travel on roads and over rough terrain. Their open cargo area can carry bales of hay or small machines, as well as farm dogs.

Horses travel to events in special horse trailers. Cattle and sheep are transported in special wagons pulled by trucks.

 The first pickup was produced in 1925. It was based on the Ford Model T car, with a modified rear body.

 Before these machines were invented farmers got around their farms on horseback. Animals were driven to markets on foot.

 Did you know some farmers use **quad bikes** to get around their farms?

 Many pickup trucks have diesel engines.

Horse trailer

23

Glossary

4x4s
Vehicles that have all four wheels powered by the engine instead of only two.

auger
A conveyor, often inside a tube, that uses a large rotating screw to move material uphill.

diesel engine
An engine that uses diesel instead of petrol for fuel.

horse-drawn
Pulled by horses.

quad bike
These vehicles look like four-wheeled motorcycles. They are used off road.

semi-trailer truck
A truck made up of a tractor unit and a removable trailer unit.

take-off shaft
A device that transfers power from one machine to another.

Total Mixed Ration
Feed that makes a perfect ration of food for cows.

Index